# Reflections of the Heart

## By

## Janis I. Soucie

**Your ISBN:**
978-0-359-37867-8

## Dedication

For God, thanks for the talent, inspiration and strength to write my story.

For Mom, may your soul and love live on through the lives of those you've touched.

For my friends, family, and church family, may our relationships endure through the coming years.

To the love of my life, Eric, thank you for staying by my side and for your unconditional love.

## Preface

People come into your life for a short time, or they may be there for the rest of your life. As a child, I felt everyone would be there forever and things wouldn't change. There was security in that thought. I had learned that people die, but when you say that to a three or four-year-old, they don't even think a loved one can die. Nope! Childhood would just go on forever. Long summer days of playing with friends, swimming in the kiddie pool, going to the zoo, the circus, the park, eating ice cream, long days at the beach. Ahhh... yep. Those are the days.

Then you wake up an adolescent and realize, childhood is not forever and your butt is about to go to college or to find a job. A whole new life is about to begin and you're not ready for it. You haven't chosen a career path or even thought about choosing one and you have no plan for your future. Yikes! That is enough stress.

But what if you are a teenager who has to care for a terminally ill parent? How does that affect your life? Your thoughts? Your emotions? Your reactions?

I can tell you, losing a parent changes everything.

I'm going to share my story with you and how God helped me through it all.

## To Say Goodbye

The stars are out tonight
They are as beautiful
As the ones I used to see in your eyes
They sparkle and gleam of their own accord
Nothing controls them
They are free
Much like you used to be

I loved that in you
The wild streak
The living on the edge perspective
But now...
Things have changed
You have changed
You are free to roam the magnificent heavens
Or Earth if you wish to stay
Your time has come
And I miss you since you departed this world
Even though it has only been a day

Wrapped tightly in a blanket
I stand here, on the edge of a jagged cliff
Shivering from the night's frosty breath
Do I end my pitiful life now?
Or do I solely go on living with only the memory of you?

Table of Contents

# CHAPTER 1

## SHADOW OF ILLNESS

*"And it shall be in the last days," God says, that I shall pour forth of My spirit on all mankind; and your sons and daughters shall prophesy, and your young men shall see visions, and your old men shall dream dreams, even on My bondslaves, both men and women, I will in those days pour forth of My spirit and they shall prophesy." Acts 2:17, 18 NASB*

The dreams of my mother's impending death began when I was about four years old. I remember one dream vividly as if I were dreaming it right now. It reoccurred, but even as a young girl I knew it had significance.

I was spending the night at my niece Jessica's house as I often did and I was fast asleep in her bed. Jessica is my sister Margie's firstborn.

In the dream, my sister Margie, came to wake me up. She told me she had something to show me and that I must go with her quickly.

I sat up slowly and groggily rubbed my eyes to clear the sleep from them. I took my sister's hand and followed her. I climbed out of bed and began to follow her down a hallway that mysteriously faded and morphed to an outdoor setting. We were walking through an old iron gate and down a gravel path with the light of the moon to guide us. There were large trees to my right and we were high on a hill.

It was windy and I was chilled. I looked down to see what I was wearing, thinking that if I had known where we were going I

2

would have dressed better. I looked at my clothing and realized I was in my everyday clothes of jeans, a T-shirt, jacket and sneakers. I don't remember having time to change.

Still holding my sister's hand, I followed her down the driveway a few more feet before I told her that I was scared.

"There's nothing to be afraid of, Janis. It'll be okay. There is something I'm supposed to show you," she said in a kind voice, the wind whipping her long, dark, wavy hair around her face.

"But I don't wanna see what you're going to show me! It's not good." I hung my head low with sadness.

"It's okay. Trust me."

"But I don't want to! I..." I stopped. There was a rumbling in the sky to our left and there came a great, deep voice.

"Janis, follow your sister. It's all right. You will be okay."

In awe, I looked up in the sky, where a bright, golden light surrounded a man with a crown. I knew who this man was as I had learned about Him in Sunday school. He was God, my Heavenly Father, and I knew I had better do what He said. And so, I trusted Him and followed my sister.

It wasn't until my sister brought me to a gravestone that I realized where I was. We were in a cemetery and before me, was a gravestone with my mother's name, birth and death date chiseled in neat letters. I couldn't make out her death date but the outline of the last three numbers showed me that they were the same.

I began to cry and shake my head. "No! Noooo! She's not dead!" I screamed in frantic tears.

My sister knelt to my level and took hold of me. "Janis, it's okay. It will be okay."

"Janis, listen to your sister," came the deep, but gentle voice. "She is telling you the truth. Everything will be all right."

I sniffled, starring up at God while my sister held me by having one hand on each arm. I didn't know what to say at first but inside I felt a calmness I couldn't explain. All I knew was that everything would be okay so long as I continued to believe that.

"Okay," I said, nodding my head and staring up at the lighted clouds. As if on accepting the words as truth and believing them, God smiled and disappeared into the clouds. The golden light dwindled until only the light of a nearly full moon accompanied us.

I awoke from this dream in tears and I screamed for my mother. I carried on until Margie called our mother who lived just next door; Margie's trailer and the farmhouse where my mom, my dad, my brothers Joel and Alex, and my sister Beth, and I lived, were on the same lot.

My mother came rushing over and she carried me home from my sister's place. She asked me why I was crying and I told her that I had a dream where she died.

Still holding me, she rubbed my back and said, "Oh, Janis. I'm not going to die."

My mother never knew it but I felt like she lied to me and I was angry with her for it. I knew someday she would die and I didn't understand why she told me otherwise. It wasn't until years later that I learned why she had told me she wasn't going to die. It never occurred to me that she might have been afraid of what I dreamed.

The dreams didn't end there. They continued for years.

One of the next dreams I remember having was when I was in my early to mid-teens.

I was on the bus ride home from school with my niece Jessica and her half-brothers Robby and Joel. Jessica was the first one off the bus and I was behind her. She ran toward the house to tell her grandma everything about her day at school. I hung back, standing in the driveway by the doors to the bus, as the bus driver and I were having a conversation. Robby and Joel bounded down the stairs and stood next to me. Everything was fine until Jessica's blood boiling scream reached my ears. I felt my muscles tense as I turned to look in her direction. She hadn't even made it inside. She paused at the bottom of the cement stairs that led to the side entrance to the house.

"Janis, come here," she screamed waving her arms frantically in a gesture for me to come to her.

"What is it?" I said not moving from my position by the bus. Her scream did scare me and I wanted to see what was wrong, but fear had managed to grip my feet and hold me firm to the ground.

4

"It's grandma! She's sick."

"What do you mean? You can't see her. She's inside," I said, unable to see if anyone was lying on the stairs as a there was a large pack of flowers growing in my line of view.

"No, she's not. She's lying on the stairs. She's holding her stomach and turning colors. Come here!"

With those words, I ran to Jessica's side. There was my mother just as Jessica had said. She was laying at an odd angle on the stairs, holding her stomach and moaning. Her slowly wrinkling skin was a pale yellowish-green. From the sad sight of her it was obvious to us that my mother was seriously ill.

"Jan, do something," Jessica pleaded.

I walked over to my mother and helped her up. I knew there was nothing I could do but help Mother inside and call someone for help.

The dream ended when I helped Mother up from the stairs. The dream reminded me of the one I had when I was four. The same sadness and foreboding lingered in my gut and made me nauseous.

Finally, after a day or two of pondering over the dream and whether I should mention it to my mother, I decided I would tell her. I felt it was important that she know so if something was wrong, she would visit a doctor and get testing done.

I went out into the kitchen to make lunch and Mother was there putting laundry in the washer. It was then I told her about my dream. She laughed at me, not in a mean way, but nonetheless I was hurt that she didn't take me seriously. After all, this was the second dream I had told her about where she either died or was fatally ill. I never told her another one of my dreams. I didn't see the use if she was just going to shrug them off.

I'm sure she knew something was wrong and just didn't want to alarm anyone in the family. Either that or she didn't want to admit it to herself.

*O Lord, how my adversaries have increased!*
*Many are rising up against me.*
*Many are saying of my soul,*
*"There is no deliverance for him in God."*

*But You, O Lord, are a shield about me,*
*My glory and the One who lifts my head*
*I was crying to the Lord with my voice,*
*And He Answered me from his holy mountain.*
*I lay down and slept;*
*I awoke, for the Lord Sustains me.*
*I will not be afraid of ten thousands of people*
*Who have shattered the teeth of the wicked.*
*Salvation belongs to the Lord;*
*Your blessing be upon Your people!*
*Psalms 3:3 NASB*

## CHAPTER 2

## HOSPITAL RUSH

*Why am I sitting here watching the news? I hate it! It's always so negative.* I looked up at my mother, sitting across from me in her plush blue chair, rocking and crocheting. Her short, black, curly hair framed her beautiful square face. Her hazel eyes glinted with a zest for life, but deeper they held many secrets.

My mother had a rough past and we rarely spoke of it. I only heard pieces of her past from others in the family. It was

6

something we did not ask her about, and didn't speak about it in her presence.

I stared at my mother in silence as I sat on the hard, cold floor, my back leaning up against the blue couch. My heart ached for my mother and what she had been through. I wish she would talk to us about it. Heck! I wish she would just talk to us! She's always so quiet, so to herself. If only she would confide in me, but then I am the youngest of the six kids. Who would confide in me? I'm seventeen; it's not like I don't know anything, or can't just listen.

Something inside pulled me to be with my mother that night. To sit with her, even if it was while the news was on. The feeling was so intense it was hard to deny and I could feel the tears brim my eyes. *Why am I feeling this way? This is insane.* I couldn't understand what I felt, but I knew I had to listen to that feeling, or I might regret not spending that time with my mother.

So, there I sat on the floor waiting for the moment my mother and I could watch Wheel of Fortune and Jeopardy together. Then the evening would grow lively as my mother and I competed in the games. I so couldn't wait!

But first, the CBS Evening News was on with Dan Rather who I liked well. I didn't like the topics of the news. They just bothered me too easily, yet somehow, I became engrossed.

The squeak of the recliner rocking tore my brown eyes from the TV set and I stared at my mother. She had put her crocheting down and bolted out of the room, her small hand covering her mouth. My heart jumped. It's all right. She probably just ate something that is bothering her. She'll feel better when she throws up, I said, trying to rationalize the incident. Listening to my own words my heart rate slowed and my muscles relaxed. I turned back to the TV and every once and a while looking to see if my mother had returned.

I wasn't watching the clock but it felt like an hour passed before I heard my mother's voice. She was talking to my father. I couldn't get every word she said but I caught something about calling her doctor. Dad told her to go ahead.

7

*Uh oh. What's wrong? Was my intuition right all along? Okay. Calm down, Janis. It might not be anything too serious. Just wait and see what happens after the phone call.*

My mother was short and overweight but she had a good spirit and a laugh I was always delighted to hear. I watched her walk into the living room and grab the Rolodex from the phone stand and sort through the cards until she came to her doctor. She dialed the number and after a few rings, she began talking to someone.

My heart was racing and my breathing more rapid and shallow. Man! I was so nervous. I couldn't imagine what my mother must have been feeling.

I watched and listened only catching one side of the conversation. "I've been throwing up bile," my mother said.

*Ewe! Totally gross! Did I want to hear this?*

"So I should go to the ER then?" My mother's tone of voice was one of "do I have to?"

A minute later, "Okay. That's what I'll do then." She hung up the phone and walked into the dining room where my father was eating dinner.

"I wasn't able to get a hold of my doctor but her assistant told me to go to the emergency room."

"Okay," he said, picking up his dinner dishes and taking them to the kitchen.

I listened as they talked in the kitchen and the sliding pantry doors opened. Half of the pantry was for food, of course, but the other half housed our coats. I looked out into the kitchen and saw Mom standing in front of Dad talking to him and zipping her coat.

I sat back on the couch staring at the TV but not paying much attention. My ears were in tune to the voices in the kitchen and then the footsteps getting closer to the living room.

"I'm taking your mom to the emergency room. It will probably be late when we get back," he said, zipping up his winter coat.

"Okay," I said, for what else could I say? There were no questions I could ask that would have answers.

I did want to go with them and be there to show Mom support, but I knew it would be late when we got back. I had no idea how long I'd be there if I went. Being in such busy places grated on my skin and made me uncomfortable. No, thank you! I'll stay home. Besides, I was certain Mom was coming home that night so what was the big deal anyway?

I stared blankly at the TV while listening to the kitchen door close as my parents left. Shortly after, I walked to the window where I saw the shadowy figures of my parents walk to the car. The car doors closed and then there was a low rumble as my dad started up the tan Ford Mercury Topaz. The headlights switched on and reflected off the glistening snowing blanketing the lawn as dad backed down the driveway. I watched the car drive down the road praying to God that everything would be all right. The sound of the car's engine faded into the cold darkness.

I sat there stunned but remained hopeful everything would be fine and mom would be sent home in a few hours.

Yet somewhere inside fear rose like smoke from kindling before it burst into flames. My heart started to pound, my body and mind becoming restless. *I must call her.*
I bolted across the room, picked up the phone and dialed my sister's number. Her husband Isaac answered.

"Hi, Jan," he said using a nickname I got when I was younger.

"Hi, is Beth there?"

"Yes, but she's busy. Can she call you back?"

*Call me back? You so have to be kidding me! I am barely keeping it together. No! I need to speak to her now.* I was feeling shaky.

"It's important," I said longing to hear my sister's voice.

Isaac was silent. I heard my sister's voice in the background.

"What is it?" Isaac asked.

I wanted to talk to Beth directly but I was so scared I had to tell someone. I couldn't wait for her to call me back.

"Mom is in the emergency room."

I listened as Isaac told Beth and then there was fumbling of the phone and then Beth's voice. "What's going on?" she asked hurriedly.

"Mom threw up earlier and called her doctor. She mentioned she was throwing up bile and wondered what she should do. She was told to go to the ER."

"Have you called the ER?"

"No. I haven't," I said, realizing I hadn't even thought of calling the hospital. Even at the thought I felt anxious about it and then ashamed for not being brave enough to call.

Beth knew I was shy and didn't press the matter. "Okay. I'll call and I will call you back."

"Okay," I said as we hung up. As I waited I suddenly realized how big and ominous our two-story, brown shingled farmhouse could be. This time of year, the cold air made its way through all the drafty places making the furnace work harder to heat the house.

I was happy the wind wasn't blowing. I couldn't stand the creaking and groaning of the house on top of everything else that was going on.

*I can't stand waiting alone like this. I need to talk to someone.* I reached for the phone and dialed my brother Alex's number. He picked up after a couple of rings.

"Hi, Alex. I was just calling to let you know that mom is in the emergency room."

"Why? What's wrong?"

"She was throwing up bile and called her doctor's office to see what she should do. They told her to go to the ER. I called Beth and she is trying to get through to the ER and find out if mom has seen the doctor yet. She said she would call me back when she finds out anything."

"Okay."

"Once she calls I'll give you a call back and keep you updated."

"Okay. Thanks for letting me know."

"You're welcome, Alex," I said using my brother's nickname. "I'll chat with you soon. Bye."

Alex and I hung up the phones and I walked back to the couch and waited to try to focus on a television show. Thankfully, it distracted me for a while. I felt like hours were slipping by but when I looked at the clock it was only about a half hour. *How much longer am I going to have to wait?* I couldn't believe how

10

nervous I felt. I feared the longer I had to wait the worse the news would be.

The phone rang and my heart skipped a beat. I was scared to answer the phone, yet I knew I needed to if I wanted to find out what was going on.

"Hello?"

"Hi, Jan. I talked to Dad and he said the doctor hasn't been in to see Mom yet," Beth said.

*That's so typical of the ER.*

"A nurse has been in to see her to take her vital signs. Mom's temperature has spiked and she is having stomach pain, gas, and nausea.

"I'll call the hospital back in a while to see if anything has changed."

"Okay, thanks."

After I hung up with Beth, I called Alex back and told him what Beth had told me. He was grateful I was keeping him informed, but we didn't talk long as I didn't know when Beth would be calling me back.

I thought about what Beth said about Mom's symptoms. I remember Mom having problems with gas and constantly saw her popping Tums. I even knew about the stomach pain. There were times I would lightly push on her stomach and she would burp. It happened every time and Mom and I both laughed. That was until one day she cried out in pain. I apologized and never pushed on her stomach again. I didn't understand why it would hurt since I didn't push on her stomach hard. I felt something was wrong, but neither Mom, or I, knew what it could be.

I turned back to the television. I tried to focus on the show but couldn't. My thoughts were bent on Mom and what might be wrong with her.

I don't remember how much time passed when the phone rang and jolted me from my thoughts.

"Hello?"

"Hi, Jan. Has Dad called?" Beth asked.

"No, he hasn't."

"Okay, I'll call the hospital again.

11

Two hours passed and the hour was approaching 11PM. I thought for sure Mom and Dad would be home by now. The longer I waited the stronger the feel grew that something was horribly wrong.

I started to doze off on the couch when Beth called me back.

"Hello?"

"Hi, Jan. I talked to Dad. The doctor has been in to see Mom and he has ordered tests. Mom's temperature is up so they are keeping her overnight for observation.

"Dad said he would be home soon."

"Okay," I said feeling bummed. I wanted Mom to be okay and come home.

I hung up with Beth and called Alex. I updated him on Mom's situation and then said good night.

I looked around for my dog, Teka, who usually sat with Mom until I went to bed. Teka always slept with me.

I found Teka and let her outside and while I waited for her to finish, I watched the darkness at the end of the driveway. I hoped that at any moment headlights would pierce through the darkness as Dad came home. But there was nothing.

Teka came running inside from the cold and I quickly shut the door. I left the porch light on for Dad for when he comes home.

I hated being alone. It was so eerie in our big old drafty farmhouse.

I felt chilled as I walked back into the living room to turn off the TV and the light by the couch. I was rarely ever alone and it just felt so awkward.

I scurried up the creaky carpeted stairs and to my room. I closed the blinds in my window, changed into pajamas, and climbed into bed. I had had enough of the evening. All I wanted was to fall asleep, have good dreams, and wake up in the morning to Mom making breakfast as she always did.

I woke up the next morning almost forgetting about the night before like it had been a dream. The conversations, the wait, and dread all rushed back. I fought getting out of bed. I was so tired but how could I go back to sleep?

Did dad come back at all last night? I didn't remember hearing him ascend the stars and enter his room. But that doesn't

12

mean he didn't come home. I listened for noises in the house and there it was, dad's voice. He was on the phone.

*I have to figure out what's going on.* I rushed around my room to get dressed and brush my hair. I walked downstairs and wanted to talk to dad so bad but he was still on the phone. I let Teka outside and made breakfast while I waited. *Oh, when is he going to be off the phone? What were the results of Mom's tests? Is she going to be okay?*

Finally, Dad hung up the phone and I walked into the living room to talk with him.

"Dad, how's Mom doing?"

"She's has to have surgery to remove gallstones blocking her bile duct."

"Is that why she was throwing up bile?" I asked, my mind churning with the new information.

"Yes. She is to have surgery early tomorrow morning."

Oh, good! Well, I mean I am relieved that all mom needed was surgery to remove the gallstones and then she would be back home and recovering in no time. Phew!

*How long, O Lord? Will You forget me forever?*
*How long will You hide Your face from me?*
*How long shall I take counsel in my soul,*
*Having sorrow in my heart all the day?*
*How long will my enemy be exalted over me?*

*Consider and answer me, O Lord my God;*
*Enlighten my eyes, or I will sleep the sleep of death,*
*And my enemy will say, "I have overcome him,"*
*And my adversaries will rejoice when I am shaken.*

*But I have trusted in Your lovingkindness;*
*My heart shall rejoice in Your salvation.*
*I will sing to the Lord,*
*Because He has dealt Bountifully with me.*
*Psalm 13 NASB*

## CHAPTER 3

## THE UNEXPECTED

January 21, 1999. I'll never forget the date. It was not only the day for Mom's surgery for the gallstones, but it was the day the lives of my loved ones would be affected in a way we didn't expect.

I imagined being in Mom's shoes and if I were, I would be a wreck! I was scared for her to go through surgery without anyone to be at the hospital to support her. Would the surgery be too much for her?

Mom is a strong person and I've seen her come through tough situations before. Yet, for reasons I didn't understand, I felt sad like this might be different.

Mom's surgery was early this morning. So, by the time we got to the hospital she was out of surgery and in recovery.

We took the elevator to the second floor and went to mom's room. I imagined her in her bed and happy knowing she had come out of surgery and would be okay. I knew she would start to feel so much better. But my heart sank when her room was empty.

Dad and I waited in her room for about a half hour or so but no one came to update us on her condition. Mom obviously needed more time in recovery.

We took the elevator down to the first floor, crossed the lobby and waiting area, and walked to the gift shop. We looked around in different areas. I looked at bookmarks knowing that mom loved to read. There were bookmarks with pennies attached to them and the pennies had a design cut out of them. The bookmark I chose was inspirational and the center of the penny was cut out in the shape of an angel.

With the bookmark in hand, I walked through the candy and food isles to an area with stuffed animals. I spotted a small brown bear holding a heart in his paws that read, "I love you".

After paying for the items, we went back up to mom's room. We didn't wait long before a tall, heavy set, female doctor in a white coat, walked in.

"Are you Betty Monroe's family?"

"Yes, we are," answered my father,

"Betty is coming out of recovery and will be brought up to her room in a few minutes.

"The surgery went well. Her gallbladder was full of stones and we had to remove it. While we were in there we did exploratory surgery and we found tumors."

*Exploratory surgery? What gave you the idea to do that?*

An alarm sounded in my head, which may as well have been the red alert sound on Star Trek the Original Series.

*Tumors! Oh no! Please, not cancer. Please say the tumors are benign.* I desperately prayed I wasn't about to receive some of the worse news in my life.

The doctor continued, "We took a few samples and sent them to the lab to find out if they cancerous or not. The tests came back positive for cancer," she said with a sorrowful expression and tone. "The cancer has spread throughout her abdomen and is in a layer across her stomach."

My mind was screaming, *Mom has cancer! No. I can't accept that. This isn't supposed to happen.*

I was focused on this terrible news and what it might mean. I zoned out and didn't hear the rest of the conversation. I felt I had drifted into another world for a while but I'm sure it was only a Matter of seconds.

When I came back to the conversation I heard, "Betty doesn't know about the cancer, but I will tell her once the anesthesia has time to wear off."

Fear bubbled up like hot tar inside me. I was overcome by the overwhelming need to cry. I needed to release the tears, but at that moment I saw my mother lying on a stretcher in the hallway, waiting to come into her room.

I wanted to be strong for her and held back the tears. Plus, I knew that if she saw me cry she would know something was wrong. I didn't want to worry her in her condition. I couldn't cry...not just yet.

Dr. Tracey asked my dad and I to leave the room so they could bring my mother into her room and get her situated. We walked out into the hallway and stood against the opposite wall.

I looked at my mother and my breath caught in my throat. Her skin was an eerie yellow like she was under strange lights. I had never seen this before and surmised that it must be how someone looked after they came out of surgery.

Aside from her coloring, mother looked peaceful lying in the stretcher, covered in a light, white blanket, her head resting on a semi-fluffy white pillow. She was still groggy and could barely open her eyes to see us. When her light blue eyes looked on my hazel eyes she gave a faint smile and I smiled. At that moment, her smile erased all fear and I felt like things would be all right after all.

I leaned up against the cool, cream colored wall as two orderlies wheeled my mother into the room. As I waited the chemical smell of cleaning agents swirled around me. *Oh, how I hate the smell of hospitals.*

My mind drifted back to the news that mom had cancer. The first thing I think of when I hear someone has cancer is that they are going to die. I don't know why I always jump to the worst conclusion. I guess it's because I know people die from cancer.

The news swam in my head. I tried to think how I could stand in front of my mother knowing something she didn't. I desperately felt she should be told about the situation she is in.

My heart pumped fiercely and my muscles tightened. How could I face my mother and say nothing? How could I stand before her and not release the slightest emotion that battled to be free?

I couldn't stay any longer. Adrenaline had me hyped up and my body was ready run out of an overwhelming situation. I needed to leave and deal with the news I received. I was so out of sorts with everything I was feeling.

I thought of asking my dad to take me home. I was always nervous talking to him so it took me a while to build up the courage to speak to him.

"Dad, can you take me home?" I asked, with tears ready to burst forth.

"Do you think you can stay a bit longer? I'd like to stay with your mother."

*Oh, he didn't just ask me that. No! I can't stay longer. Why do you think I asked to leave? Ugh!*

I could barely handle the situation as it was. I was not happy, but at the same time I understood. My dad was my ride home, so if he stayed, I stayed. I was struggling and I think my dad knew this.

"Maybe you can get a ride home with your brother Joel when he comes to visit?" my dad suggested.

I didn't say anything. I felt defeated and turned inward. *I can't believe you want me to wait for my brother to get here. I don't even know when he's getting here!*

I was so frustrated and hurt. My dad was asking me to wait even though I was struggling to deal with my emotions. He didn't even console me or ask how I was doing or anything like that. I needed someone to talk to and I was desperate.

I stared at the floor lost in thought. I looked up when I heard footsteps approach. Dr. Tracey walked out of Mother's room and stopped in front of us. "She's all settled know. She is still groggy but you can go in and see her.

"Thank you," said my father with a dull tone.

The doctor gave a faint smile, nodded, and walked away.

*I'm not sure I'm ready for this.* I hung back in the hallway and let dad go into the room first. It wasn't that I didn't want to see mom. It was just that I was horribly scared of the predicament my mother was in and I felt if I wasn't near her, I wouldn't be forced to deal with it. I guess that was a way to comfort myself, not that it helped very much.

I followed Dad into Mom's room. He walked over to the right side of her bed and stood there looking at her with bridled emotions. Daylight flooded the room from the large windows behind him. The brightness of the day helped to lift my spirits a little like hope rode in on the light.

I sat in a chair that was next to the wall at the foot of Mom's bed. I wanted to give her the things I bought her but she was in and out of consciousness. I thought it best to wait.

I stared at my mother, my own tears stifled, when I saw how yellow her skin had turned. I wasn't sure why this had happened. I just prayed to God that she would be all right.

I found out later that mom's blocked gallbladder had caused jaundice, or yellowing of the skin. If she didn't have the surgery when she did she may not have lived to see tomorrow morning. What a scary thought!

Lost in my inner world, I lost track of time. When I looked at my mother lying in the hospital bed before me I felt uncertainty and then security flew out the window. It was an unsettling feeling. I was seventeen with low self-esteem and my "safety" person was ill with cancer. *I can't lose her! I just can't! If she does die, what will I do without her?*

Mom's light blue eyes opened; I was so glad she was awake. She was able to stay awake for a while and I was so happy to show her what I bought her. She smiled when I showed her the bear holding the heart that said, "I love you". Oh, how I loved to see that contagious, room-brightening smile again. For a moment, I felt everything would be fine.

Family members began to arrive by early afternoon. I watched from my chair as Dad took each person out into the hall. I knew what he was doing. He was telling them Mom had cancer. He asked them to keep the news a secret and told them mom didn't know yet. The more people he took aside the more real the situation became.

My dad's sisters Arletha and Margie were there along with Margie's husband Ronnie. We all stood around in my mother's room, knowing a secret and wondering how much longer we had to keep it.

The day had matured and it was late afternoon, Dad and I hadn't had anything to eat in several hours. I looked at my father and thought, *I am so hungry. When are we going to get something to eat?*

I didn't ask my father if we could get something in the cafeteria. I mean, he wouldn't take me home, so there was nothing that made me think he would leave Mom's side for a short while to get food.

I sat silently in my chair, observing the room and then the people in it. The atmosphere of the room was ominous and eerie during moments of silence.

My Aunt Art approached my father, "Have either of you had lunch?"

"No, we haven't," my father answered.

"Why don't we go to the cafeteria? Margie and Ronnie will stay here with Betty.

My father was reluctant. He looked at my mother and I could see the forlorn in his brown eyes at the thought of leaving her. Then his brown eyes settled on my hazel eyes. He must have seen the pleading in my eyes just as I hoped he would. "All right, he said with a sigh.

The three of us walked to the cafeteria, got a tray of food, and sat down. I was so happy to finally have something to eat, but

19

better yet I was away from my mother's room. Being in a near empty cafeteria was like stepping outside the hospital and standing in fresh air. I was out of the sad atmosphere of mother's room and felt I could relax, breathe and more easily set my mind on happier things. It was like I could easily fool myself into thinking my mother was just recovering from gallbladder surgery and nothing more.

I ate quickly as my dad and aunt talked. "The thing I'm wondering is how much insurance is going to pay for," said my dad a concerned look on his face.

I glanced away from my dad, sadness tugging at my heart. The talk of insurance only reminded me of the severity of the situation. But then the talk of finances... Ugh! It drove me nuts. My parents were always talking and worrying about finances since I was young.

The thing is they taught me to trust God, that He would provide for all our needs. I just couldn't understand why my dad couldn't have faith God would provide again. He has always come through in the past and has never failed us. I didn't believe God would abandon us. After all, I was taught that He is a loving God, and a loving God would never walk away from His children.

When we were finished, we took care of our trays and headed back to the elevator. We rode up to mom's floor, got off and walked back into her room.

By six in the evening, the room grew crowded as more visitors, mostly family, poured in. Among them were my sister Margie and her husband, brothers Alex and Joel. Joel came with his wife and their daughter Stephanie; Kylie was also pregnant with their second child. As each group came in, Dad took them aside and relayed the bad news. Everyone was shocked as would be expected. They were asked not to say anything of course. The doctor would be in soon to finally tell my mother she had cancer.

Everyone chatted about work and what was going on in their personal lives. I sat quiet most of the time just listening and observing. I never was much of a talker. I had my own inner world that I would only share with a select few.

I felt so alone and isolated in a room full of people. My body was urging me to leave, but I couldn't. I'm not much of an introvert, am I? Ha! Give me the solitude of my room, a journal to

20

write in and prayer time with God any day. I would only emerge if I felt ready to and then return to my room when I had my fill of social stimulation.

If only I could do that now. That's one reason I hated not having my license and my own car. I was at someone else's mercy to take me somewhere and until they decided to leave, I was trapped. At least that's how I felt.

I looked up as a tall hefty woman entered the room and stood by my mother's bedside. It was the doctor. The time had come for her to tell my mother the bad news.

"Betty, now that you're more awake and your family is with you, I'd like to tell you how your surgery went," said Dr. Tracey.

"Okay," my mother replied in a weak voice.

"The surgery went well. We had to remove your gallbladder because it was impacted with gallstones.

"After we removed your gallbladder, we did some exploratory surgery and found tumors lying like a blanket across your belly. We did a biopsy and sent it to the lab. Betty, you have cancer," the doctor said in a sorrowful tone.

We all watched Mom's expression all expecting her to cry but her face stayed emotionless as she said, "I know. I had expected it."

We were all quiet and thought of the surgery she had yet to go through. It would be in February so not too far away. I was nervous. But I prayed everything would be okay.

## CHAPTER 4

## INTO THE O.R.

It's hard to believe just twelve days ago mom had her gallbladder out and we found out she had cancer.

Here it is February and today, Dad, Mom, Aunt Art and I traveled to Syracuse for Mom's pre-op testing and evaluation. What a horrible day it was to see my mother in such pain as we strolled the sidewalks of the city.

Mother stopped walking several times. She held her stomach and said, "I can't do this. It hurts too much."

"Betty, you have to get to your doctor's office. It's closer than our car," said my father wanting to help her but not sure how.

Mom must have felt encouraged because she took another step toward the doctor's office. But again she stopped and was crying in pain. "I can't go any further," she said holding her stomach. My dad was on one side of her and my Aunt on the other.

"Okay. We'll see if we can find you a wheelchair," my dad said looking around the buildings. He was searching for a medical building that way he would be sure to get a wheelchair.

While he did this, I looked around our little area for a place for us to rest, but there was no place for us to sit.

Finally, dad came back with a wheelchair and wheeled mom to her doctor's office. My mom checked in and sat down in the waiting room. My Aunt and I did the same while my dad took the wheelchair back to the medical facility he borrowed it from.

I stayed with mom and Aunt Art in the waiting room. There were plenty of people in there and it took mom a while to be seen. Finally, she was called in. My Aunt and I continued to sit in the waiting room. My dad came in.

"Where's your mother?"

"She was called back to see the doctor."

"Oh. I had wanted to go with her."

"You probably still can," said my Aunt. "Just go to the counter and tell them you are Betty Monroe's husband and you wish to be in the appointment with her.

My dad was reluctant to do this. He always seemed shy in some instances. He sat down and waited for a while and then eventually went up to the reception area to get an update on my mother and how things were going.

A woman told her she was having a rough time and crying, but that she would be out soon. It was maybe a half hour later when my mother and her doctor came into the waiting area. Mother was in tears and red faced. I just wanted to hug her and wish that my hug could heal her. I had hoped that the doctor would give her something for the pain. Mother even asked him but he said no. *How cruel! Here she was suffering from cancer eating away at her and you won't give her some pain pills to help relieve the pain so she can be more comfortable while she waits for surgery! Stupid doctor!*

Oh, yes. I was angry and I just pictured myself rushing up to the doctor and giving him a piece of my mind. Of course I didn't.

We were all upset at the doctor. We just couldn't understand how he could not see how much pain she was in? She was fifty-seven years old and a mother of six who was not on narcotics and didn't have a history of addiction. So why not give her something? Ugh!

We left the doctor's office and helped my mother walk back to the car. It was rough for her but she was a trooper through it all. Once mother was in the van, the rest of us climbed in and dad

23

drove us to the Carousel Mall, parking near the food court entrance. We were all past ready for lunch. After lunch, we headed home.

It was a long day for all of us but especially for my mother. It took us about an hour to get to Syracuse not counting traffic time, then all the pain she endured, and then having to make the hour or so trip back home. She was exhausted.

Today is February 14th. Tomorrow will be a long day. I don't really have any bad feelings about the trip or the surgery. I think everything will be fine, yet there is something that is still bothering me like there is more to Mom's condition than we are aware of. Well, something along that line anyway.

The trip to Syracuse will take about an hour, maybe longer because we will be driving in the early morning when many people will be on their way to work. I am anxious about seeing the hospital where I was born, but oh, how I wish it could be under happier circumstances.

I cut up some carrots and celery and put them in sandwich bags as snacks for the trip. I took a drink as well. Who knew, with everything that was going on, when we would be able to stop and get something to eat or drink. At least I would have some nutrients in my system.

I can't imagine how Mom must have felt today. All day long she had to drink this special liquid that would help clean out her system. Plus she couldn't have much of anything to eat or drink unless it was clear like Jell-O or water. Being her sole caretaker, I had to help give her the nasty stuff. Mom also had to consume a potassium drink to help get her potassium levels up so her heart would be strong to endure surgery. She didn't care for it and on the first few sips she gagged and threw it back up. Good thing we had a small bucket there for her. I couldn't get her to drink anymore. I was praying her heart was strong enough for surgery.

February 15th. Sunrise. How little of these I have seen. I'm not usually a morning person but this morning I had to be. I would be riding with my sister Margie to take Mom to Syracuse for her cancer surgery. Dad, Aunt Art, Aunt Margie and Uncle Ronnie would be going as well. Aunt Margie and Uncle Ronnie would be going down in their own car as they won't be staying in Syracuse like Dad, Aunt Art, Margie and I will be.

We all had gotten up early, had breakfast and now we were running around trying to get things situated and ready for the trip.

Mom's bed was in the living room as she had a hard time walking up the stairs; it hurt her stomach too much. I had noticed that before she went into the hospital in January, that it would take her longer to go up and down stairs then it normally would.

Most everyone was in the living room trying to help Mom get ready and just chatting with her.

"Janis, can you go upstairs and get your mother some clothes?" asked my dad.

I didn't say anything and quietly ran up the stairs knowing I was operating in a limited time frame before we had to leave.

I entered Mom's room and turned on the light. I went to her dresser and started searching for the clothes she needed. *I don't know what Mom wants to wear. What if I pick something she doesn't like?*

I don't know if anyone else would have thought what Mom wanted at a time like this. They just focused on getting her to her appointments on time. Did anyone besides myself, think about what she might be thinking or feeling? I can't imagine this was easy to go through.

I searched through Mother's dresser drawers for all the items of clothing she would need. I felt I was doing the best I could when I heard, "Janis, you need to hurry up," my Dad yelled upstairs. I couldn't go any faster and I was doing what I could under the level of stress I was under. Couldn't he understand? If he wanted me to hurry so badly, why didn't someone come upstairs and help me?

With my arms full of clothes, I ran downstairs and into the living room. I emptied my arms on Mom's bed and she began to get undressed. Everyone, including Margie's husband Tim, was there in the living room as Mom undressed. I felt so sorry for her having to change in front of everyone like that. I wanted to chase everyone out of the room so as to pay her some respect and

25

privacy. I know if I was her I would want my privacy, but then Mother was the kind of person who wasn't afraid to do things others might never find the courage to do. There is so much you think would bother her but it doesn't. At least she doesn't show it.

After Mom was dressed and everyone was loading things into the car, I quickly packed up the snacks and drinks I had prepared for the day and headed outside into the bitter cold air. I hopped into the back of Margie's gray Oldsmobile and buckled myself in. Margie, of course, was behind the wheel, the car idling, and Mother was in the passenger seat. I couldn't help but to wonder how long Mom would be able to handle the ride as she was having unexpected bouts of diarrhea. There had been a couple of times she wasn't able to make it to the bathroom. I had to help my sister clean up one mess. Something I never thought I would have to do.

Margie had her window down and she was talking to Dad and Aunt Art who were parked in the driveway next to her. They were making sure Aunt Art and Margie had each other's cell phone numbers so we could keep in contact and let each other know if we needed to make a stop. When everything was settled, we were off, driving east on Sulphur Springs road toward I-81 south.

Most of the drive down was sunny and uneventful. The view out the windows was the highway which was lined by trees. The closer we came to Syracuse the fewer trees we saw and a transition to more suburban culture.

We had to make a couple of stops for Mom and one time we had to pull off the Interstate and try and find a place as quick as possible. Margie pulled over and tried to call Aunt Art and let them know we were going to find a place with a restroom, but we didn't have any luck and we watched out the windows as Dad, Aunt Art, Aunt Margie and Uncle Ronnie drove by us.

It wasn't easy but we did manage to find a gas station. I walked inside with Mom and, of course, the bathroom wasn't inside the store. We had to wait in line for the key and then make our way back outside to the side of the store. Thankfully, the bathroom was free and Mom didn't have to wait any longer. She got into the bathroom just in time.

A short time later, we arrived at the hospital. We stopped outside the doors where they received patients. Mom was helped out of the car; it's very painful for her to walk anymore and she had a hard time even moving out of the van.

An orderly pushed a wheel chair out through the hospital doors and up to the car. Mom was helped into the wheel chair and then was pushed inside the hospital.

Dad and I went inside with Mom while Margie and Aunt Art parked the vehicles. Checking Mom in didn't take too long. While they were getting her ready to go upstairs for surgery, Margie and Aunt Art walked in. We walked with Mom and the orderly to the left into a long hallway. We stopped at an elevator but it was for patient use only. I wanted to go *with* Mom, but instead I stood in the hallway watching her disappear behind the closing elevator doors.

Before going upstairs, my Aunt Art, Margie and I made a quick trip into the restroom. I had such a mix of emotions I wasn't sure how to feel. I was excited to see the hospital where I was born, but I was sad about my mom and what she was here for. Yet, I had a strange kind of peace, which I knew for certain came from God. How else could I find peace in a situation such as this?

When we all reconvened in the hallway, we walked down to the end of the hallway where there was an elevator to our right. We hopped inside and rode up a couple of floors. We climbed off the elevator and turned left down another hallway. (Hospitals are so full of seemingly endless hallways and I often feel like I'm in a maze.)

We passed one nurses station and then another and finally came to a waiting room where we were told to wait as they were prepping Mom for surgery. I sat next to Margie and waited in silence for when we would be able to go in and see Mom. I was glad I brought my snacks in with me. I sure was getting hungry. I wasn't used to eating breakfast so early and boy, I sure couldn't wait for lunch.

While we waited, Aunt Margie and Uncle Ronnie walked in. I'm not sure what happened but they ended up way behind us in traffic. The six of us waited in the sitting area for about a half an hour or so before we were finally let in to see Mom. She was dressed in the traditional hospital gown and was lying on a hospital bed, covered up with a thin white blanket. She had a clip on her right index finger that looked much like a clothespin only there was a wire coming out of it; the wire lead up to a machine where it monitored the oxygen level in her blood. Every once in a while, a nurse would come in and see how Mom was doing and to take her blood pressure.

As we sat there, three of us were allowed into see Mom at a time, Mom said she had to use the restroom. We weren't sure what to do as Mom was hooked up to a machine, and more often than not, she was in too much pain to move. We called a nurse in and she asked Mom if she wanted to try and use the bed pan again. I would be so embarrassed to use one of those things in front of my family but it didn't bother Mom at all. She tried to use the bed pan but nothing happened. She has been doing this a lot. She feels like she has to go but all it is, is a feeling. I can't imagine how frustrating this must be for her.

I just felt so sad seeing her lying there, helpless and knowing there was nothing I could do to make her all better so she wouldn't have to go through surgery. I wanted to save her but I couldn't.

I stayed in the room the whole time, only Dad and Margie switched on and off to let someone else come in and visit for a short time.

Before long it was time...Time for Mother to be wheeled away from us and into a room where she would be surrounded by strangers and put to sleep. We all followed Mom as she was wheeled toward the operating room. Outside the operating room doors, we had to stop and let Mom go in alone.

"Darrell, I don't want to go," Mom said, beginning to cry as she reached out for Dad. "I'm scared."

Dad walked over to her and grabbed hold of her small, smooth hand with his large, rough workman's hands. "It'll be okay. We'll be right here waiting for you."

I wanted to rush right over and give Mom a great big hug and tell her exactly what Dad did, but I feared I might make it harder for her to go through surgery if she saw the worry in my hazel eyes. I held myself back and stifled any notion to console her, which was extremely hard to do.

After Dad calmed Mom down, she was wheeled away and vanished behind the large, white swinging doors of the operating room.

Dad, Aunt Art, Aunt Margie and Uncle Ronnie, Margie, and I took the elevator back downstairs to the lobby where we were directed to a waiting area for those waiting for someone to come out of surgery.

I found a nice comfy couch to relax on. Aunt Art sat next to me on my right and Aunt Margie and Uncle Ronnie sat next to her. Margie and Dad were to my left, sitting in separate chairs. To occupy us, there was a television in the room though I didn't pay much attention to it as I would rather read through the slew of magazines made readily available.

Time passed slowly and I found it increasingly difficult to concentrate on reading anything, even if it was of great interest. My thoughts were geared toward Mom and rightly so. All I could imagine was what it was like in the operating room and how everything was going in there. Was everything going well, according to how it was planned? Regardless of my thoughts, I knew Mom wasn't completely alone. God was with her and that provided a great measure of comfort but I was still concerned with how she was doing.

From magazine to magazine I flipped, and if I wasn't trying to stay engrossed in articles and pictures to help pass the time away, I was observing others in the waiting area and found myself wondering what they were going through and who it was in their family that was sick.

A couple of long hours passed and finally Dr. A., the same doctor Mom saw in Watertown, appeared wearing a typical long white coat.

# CHAPTER 5

## THE LONG HAUL

"Are you Betty Monroe's family?" he said looking at us with a rather plain face.

"Yes. We are," Dad said, eager, like the rest of us, to hear any type of news even if it wasn't good.

"I just wanted to let you know Betty came through the surgery all right. She is being moved to recovery right now and you will be able to see her in about an hour.

"The cancer was covering most of her abdomen and even though I removed most of it, the cancer is growing fast. She is in the latest stages of ovarian cancer.

"When she gets back to Watertown, she will have to undergo chemotherapy to kill the remaining cancer cells." Dr. A., a tall thin man, held the poise of a sorrowful expression. His eyes were sad and sympathetic.

This was all I pretty much remember hearing. The chances of my mother dying were even more realistic than before. My mind was not only on Mom but on food. I was starving and I hadn't eaten anything since breakfast early this morning. All I wanted was to get lunch and then go and see "Ma", as we often called her.

Dr. A. and Dad talked for a bit away from everyone else and when they were finished the doctor walked off.

Dad stood before us and asked what we wanted to do next while we waited to see Mom. Thankfully, with it being after one in the afternoon, the unanimous decision was to go and get lunch.

So we were off to find the hospital cafeteria. I don't even really remember how to get there it was so confusing. Sure glad I wasn't alone. I would probably freak out if I got lost in a hospital, especially if Mom found out I was lost somewhere in the hospital she would not take the news well. I refused to go anywhere in the hospital by myself, well at least this hospital. It's so huge and I don't think I can even begin to compare it. I'm from the country side and I haven't seen too many large buildings, but when I do I am in awe and my mind just goes blank.

Lunch...yes. That is where we were, standing outside of the lunch room, waiting for everyone to get together as some of us needed a bathroom break. Once the group was together, walked into the cafeteria, which was a mess as remodeling was being done. There were large sheets of plastic hanging all over the place and grayish-white dust layering most areas of the floor.

I waited for Dad and Margie to go ahead of me as I was too uncertain to go first. I mean, I knew what to do, grab a tray, step up to the buffet-like counter and let the people behind the counter know what I wanted and they would kindly regard my wishes. But I hesitated and found it easier, as with most things, to let someone else go first and I would follow. I always found it hard to do much of anything especially if I was uncertain about it. I know everyone hesitates to do things sometimes, but there are times if I hesitate too long to do something I wind up not doing what I was hesitating to do. Mom knew about this and in fact, she told my brother Joel about this when one day he asked:

"What's wrong with her? Why won't she wrestle?"

"Because she was born with a condition where she hesitates longer than other people."

It was a shock to me when I heard this and for some reason Mom never made it a point to talk to me about it.

And so, the truth of her words was evident every day and so it was when we were at the hospital. I always felt like something was wrong with me because I noticed I just couldn't do things like other people. Everyone else always seemed fearless as where I would always hang back and tend to assess the situation before acting upon it, if I would act at all. Perhaps it is good in a sense

31

but in other instances it is frustrating like when I hesitate about something so simple as getting lunch for myself, or even getting up to use the bathroom. This "condition" was so much easier for me to deal with Mom around. I knew she understood me as where I didn't see how anyone else could understand. Mom was the closest to me in the family.

I stood there in line, ogling the different kinds of food, most of which were my favorite, like different kinds of pasta. I didn't take as much food as I'd like or even the kinds of food I wanted. I just couldn't seem to voice my desires but what was even harder was trying to voice my hesitation. Any time I tried I would end up frustrated because the hesitation would win out and still nothing would be said. So often I would be asked why I don't talk much and it's not that I didn't want to say something, I either didn't have anything to say or I just couldn't seem to say what I wanted to. And now...I just wanted to hurry up and get out of the line, so I could just end this, at least for the moment. I knew I would deal with this hesitation issue again later in the day.

I quickly went through the line and then made it over to a buffet counter where I could get my own food. The hesitation was less this time around but I still dealt with it to a degree. I grabbed a roll and few other contents and walked into another room where we had to pay for our meal. This was so different than the hospital cafeteria in Watertown. I was nervous and really just wanted to sit down already.

Margie went ahead of me and paid for her lunch. I wanted to follow right behind her but Dad ended up behind me and I had to wait for him so he could pay for my lunch. I didn't want to get up to the register and have the female cashier expect me to pay for my lunch. I mean, if she expected me to pay her with air, sure I could do that.

Anxiously, I waited for Dad near the register. I must have looked very uncertain as I was constantly shifting my feet or pacing around. I was a very uncertain person, seeing everyday how different I am than most people. Being in a hospital never helps and only increases the nervousness; usually if you're in a hospital it is rarely for a good reason.

Thankfully, Dad didn't take too much longer and he paid for our lunches. Margie had found a long rectangular table near the wall that was empty and Dad and I joined her. Aunt Art, Aunt Margie and Uncle Ronnie joined us shortly after.

The conversations held were about Mom and about what was going on in everyone's life. The general over-the-table chit chat. I was the only who barely said a word. I tend to be more of a listener and thinker and preferred to absorb what everyone else was saying.

About an hour passed this way and one by one we finished eating our lunch. When it was decided we should all go and see if Mom had made it to her room, we took care of our trash and trays and made our way toward the elevator. Dad knew where we were going and had told us.

We rode the elevator up a few floors and then got off. To our left and straight ahead was a small waiting room with windows that went from the ceiling half way down the walls. It was odd and I felt like I was boxed in or something and I didn't like it too well. The room was almost too small for my comfort as I am mildly claustrophobic.

I heard babies crying down the hall to my left and I learned that we were on the same floor as the maternity ward. Mom was in a room down the hall to my right, at the opposite end. I found this ironic as the last time that Mom and I were here together was when I was born about, seventeen years prior. Now, together, we are both here again, though for a far more different reason.

A hospital authority came to speak to us and said that Mom was doing all right but that she was still rather groggy. We were allowed to go in two at a time and only for short time.

We stayed there for about two more hours, most of the time spent in the waiting room. Then it came time to say our good byes to Mom and make our way to the hotel we were staying at instead of going home. Aunt Margie and Uncle Ronnie weren't staying and they left to go back to their home in Lowville, New York.

We told Mom that we had to go as we still needed to check into the hotel. We also wanted her to get her rest. We assured her that we would be back to see her tomorrow and she was glad as she told us she didn't want to be alone in the hospital. I completely understood how she felt. I didn't want to leave her there. I would have been willing to spend the night with her but I knew nurses and doctors wouldn't allow it.

Regretfully, we all left the hospital and made our way into the parking lot. Dad and Aunt Art rode together while I rode with Margie. We drove around the city until we came to our hotel, the Grand Tulip Gennessee Inn. We left our luggage in the car and walked in together. We checked in at the desk; Dad and Aunt Art had separate rooms while Margie and I had to share a room. Margie also made other arrangements as she would have to go home in a couple of days to go into work but then she and I would be coming back. Once we were all set and had the keys to our rooms, we walked up a couple of short flights of stairs and found our rooms. We had to check them out first of course and in Margie's and my room, which I thought was really nice, there was a queen bed we had to share. Margie wasn't too happy but it really didn't bother me. I already knew in advance that she and I would be sharing a room as Dad and Aunt Art had made the reservations.

After we surveyed our rooms, we went out to the vehicles and grabbed our stuff. I was happy to be out of the hospital and away from the strange odors hospitals tend to carry; I could finally breathe fresh air. Even though I was happier away from the hospital, I still wanted to go back. I felt bad for Mom being in such a large place in the midst of strangers. I wasn't worried about the kind of care she would get. Crouse has been known for good care-taking. I was more concerned with her emotional state and how much more she could endure. I wanted to be there in case she needed someone to talk to or lean on. I didn't know if I would be much help, but that didn't matter. I just wanted to be there by her bedside.

When we finished unloading our bags and suitcases, we headed down to the hotel restaurant but they were closed. We had to go to dinner but we weren't sure where to go. We eventually found a place to eat and then got gas and found somewhere to get ice cream.

The rest of the night we spent in our rooms. Margie and I watched the weather channel. There is a storm system coming through in the next day or two and she and I may be on the road when it hits. I hope it won't be too bad. At one point, while

34

watching TV, we went down to the vending machines to get a couple of sodas and snacks. We ordered a movie to watch, *The Waterboy*, with Adam Sandler, but it was almost over with. Glad I got to see part of it though. I like Adam Sandler.

After it was over with, Margie and I went to bed. I wasn't sure how well I would sleep, but I knew it had been a pretty long day and emotionally I was wiped out.


Margie and I woke up rather early this morning. She took a shower and after she was finished, we packed up our things and put them in the car. We went back inside and once we didn't see Dad or Aunt Art in the restaurant for breakfast, climbed two small flights of stairs and knocked on their bedroom doors. They were pretty much ready to go downstairs for breakfast.

Dad, Margie, Aunt Art and I ate breakfast in the hotel restaurant before going to the hospital. The breakfast was laid out buffet style with pancakes, French toast, scrambled eggs...You name it, and it was there! The food was really good and I made sure to have coffee to help me stay awake. I was happily full by the time we were ready to leave.

At the hospital, we went in to see Mom but we weren't able to stay long as she was just about to get a sponge bath. We were ushered out of the room and spent a lot of time waiting in that claustrophobic, white-walled room we were in yesterday. While we waited, Aunt Margie and Uncle Ronnie appeared in the hallway. They saw us and walked into the room. We told them what was going on and they then found seats and waited with us.

While we waited, I thought of how Margie and I would be leaving today. We would stop in and see Mom first but we wouldn't be staying too long. Margie has to go into work tomorrow. She works on Fort Drum in the Oil Analysis lab along with my brothers, Joel and Alex. We are planning on coming back the next day though. I despised the thought of leaving Mom here but then a day away from all of the monotony seemed fine with me. I felt bad that Mom just couldn't walk away from it.

After a while, two or three of us at a time were allowed to go into Mom's room. I believe Dad and Aunt Art went in first and while I waited for my turn, I thumbed through and read pieces of numerous magazines. Some were on parenting so I didn't really bother with those. I chose others like *People* or *Time*.

Eventually I was able to go in and see Mom. I clammed up as I stood at the foot of her bed. I was nervous and shy, but why I was this way around my mom? I don't know. I didn't really know what to say that would help her feel better. Yeah, there were numerous lines I could say that would comfort her in a sense, but I questioned their validity in how they could really make her feel better. Like for instance, "You'll pull through this. You're a strong woman." True on both counts, but what if Mom didn't believe this herself, and what if she didn't want to pull through this? I knew no Matter what I said, it really all depended on how Mom felt about the situation, and how she felt would determine the strength she would put forth into fighting for her life.

I slowly walked over to Mom's bedside and gave her a hug, trying to be careful not to lose my balance. I never knew how hard it was giving someone a hug while they were lying down.

Mom was still hooked up to an IV and a catheter. I had no idea what a catheter was until yesterday when I first saw Mom hooked up to it. I think it's really gross but I know it helps her so she doesn't have to keep slowly climbing out of bed to go to the bathroom. It would be too painful for her after such extensive surgery.

Mom looked at me and Margie, her hazel eyes showing her growing weariness and desperate desire to leave the hospital. Margie told Mom that we would be leaving today and Mom lightly protested: "Nooo! I don't want to be left here alone."

"It's okay, Mom. Dad and Aunt Art will be here. I have to go into work tomorrow but Jan and I will be back on Friday."

At Margie's reassuring words, Mom relaxed a bit.

I'm not sure how long Margie and I stayed in there to talk to Mom, but before we left we said our good byes. From Mom's room we walked into the waiting room and told everyone we were going to be leaving. We all exchanged words and hugs and then left Crouse Irving Memorial.

36

Margie and I made it out of Syracuse all right, but the storm we were tracking last night hit us while we were driving on I-81 North. Visibility wasn't that great as it was compounded by wet snow and wind. Thankfully, there weren't very many cars on the road. The trip home usually would take us just under an hour but we were a little bit later than that because of the weather. With God guiding us we made it home safely.

How weird it was to walk into a large, empty house by myself. It felt awkward and I had no idea how I would fare sleeping alone in the house.

Last night wasn't so bad sleeping in the house by myself. I had my Chihuahua, Tea Cup and black and white cat, Sox, with me, so they kept me company.

Didn't do too much today other than relax and wrote in my journal, which is nothing fancy, just a plain notebook. I am getting quite a collection of journals now, but they mostly consist of dreams I've decided to write down as so many of them have come true.

Margie called from work and said that when we go back to Syracuse tomorrow, she wouldn't be going in to see Mom. She has a cold and doesn't want to get Mom sick. We would be leaving tonight after she got home.

I told Margie I was nervous as I didn't think I'd remember how to get up to Mom's floor all by myself. And then I asked her how I would be getting around to the hospital and then back to the hotel. She told me that the hospital has a shuttle I could ride.

*No way!* was all I could think at first. *You want to let me travel around Syracuse all by myself? I think not!*

In my opinion, Syracuse was too big for a seventeen-year-old, country girl to be going around by herself. Perhaps I was just scared of not having the emotional and moral support should I need it. I didn't know how I would handle facing Mom alone. With other people in the room she wouldn't focus on me, so I knew she wouldn't be able to see the emotion through my facial expressions.

Margie decided that she would drive me to the hospital and then walk me up to Mom's floor but that was as far as she was going. This helped a bit, but still I would have to face Mom alone. I think that scared me more than being by myself in such a large place.

I eventually told Margie I didn't want to do it.

"Come on, Jan. You're the only who can go and see her right now." She said, gently trying to coax me into it as she didn't want to leave Mom in Syracuse all by herself. (Dad and Aunt Art were coming home tonight.) She had also told Mom that we were going to be there and she wanted to keep her word. She really didn't want to have to call Mom and tell her that we wouldn't be coming. Still, I told her I couldn't do it. I felt way too overwhelmed with this on my shoulders and I was starting to stress out. Wasn't it enough that I had been taking care of Mom when she was home and now this was placed on my shoulders as well? It was hard enough being someone's caretaker and having to withhold emotions in fear it would upset the person. It would also show weakness, that maybe I couldn't handle the job and someone else would have to step in and take my place.

I know Margie was disappointed with me and as soon as she called Mom and told her, Mom would be disappointed in me as well. I did feel bad, but at the same time I had faith that she would be all right.

Later, after Dad and Aunt Art came home, was something else. Margie was off from work and thus relayed the news that we wouldn't be going down to see Mom tonight. The general question was "Why not?" She told them and of course what was so troubling to me wasn't such a big deal to Dad and Aunt Art. Half the time I just felt like no one understood me. No one except Mom and even now I was having a hard time talking to her because I knew she was going through a lot of stuff on her own.

Dad wasn't too happy with me as now Mom would be staying in Syracuse by herself, with no one to be there with her. If he and Aunt Art had known sooner, they might have been able to stay another night.

What a sour day for me. Yeah, I knew Mom needed support but geeze, what about me? I need someone too. I was going through a lot and no one bothered to ask how I was doing, or if it was too much for me.

# CHAPTER 6

## REALITY SETTLES IN

March 7th. Mom had chemo visit today. Mom wasn't looking forward to going in for her chemo treatment. By the distraught look on her face I could tell she'd rather not go. Reluctantly, I helped her get ready for her appointment. She was dressed and ready to go with the exception of not having enough time for breakfast. We had Carnation Instant Breakfast shake mixes and I asked Mom if she wanted me to make one up for her. She said I might as well. With the shake, she'd at least have something in her stomach.

So I mixed up milk and the shake mix in one of Mom's tall Tupperware glasses with a lid and handed it to Mom as she walked out the door.

I stayed home and waited for Mom to come home. Sometime in the early afternoon I received a phone call from I believe Dad. He said Mom had an allergic reaction to an antibiotic they gave her *before* she was even able to receive chemo. They were rushing by ambulance to the hospital.

I was alarmed at what had happened. It was so unexpected and I was scared. I only hoped that the reaction wasn't really bad and that Mom would be okay.

Sometime later, Aunt Art stopped by with Uncle Ritchie and they drove me to the hospital. We all went in to see Mom together. I sat in a chair against the wall at the foot of Mom's bed. Aunt Art and Uncle Ritchie did the same. Dad sat in a chair by Mom's bed.

I guess the doctor Mom had didn't have the proper bedside manner. Dad was going on about how rude the doctor was.

I was sad looking at Mom. I didn't know what to say so I sat silent most of the time.

The doctor came in at one point, and I saw that Dad was right. The doctor was rude. Mom even broke down in tears. I'm sure the way doctor treated her, the stress of her health, and the effect of the allergic reaction was quite overwhelming for her. I couldn't imagine being in her situation and trying to handle all of the physical, mental and emotional aspects.

At one point, while Mom was crying, she said something to the effect that she didn't see why she should go through with the chemo because, "I'm just going to die anyway".

I just stared at her, looking straight into her hazel eyes in astonishment. I couldn't believe what she had just said. Those words, "I'm just going to die anyway" stung my heart and I knew Mom was giving up the fight for her life. I felt fear well up inside me. With Mom giving up, I knew she was just going to let the cancer take her.

Mom saw me crying and she looked surprised that I was crying. I don't think she expected her words to affect me as much as they did.

Aunt Art leaned in next to me and asked me if I was all right. I told her I wasn't and that I couldn't believe Mom was just going to give up. Aunt Art did her best to reassure me that Mom was just tired and she had just been through an allergic reaction. I guess Aunt Art was trying to make it like Mom wasn't *actually* going to give up. This calmed me down for the time being though there was a warning within me at the words Mom had spoken. I just couldn't shake them.

We stayed until visiting hours were over and then we went home. The doctors are keeping Mom overnight just to make sure she is going to be all right.

Mom is doing rather well today. She is sitting up in her chair and acting like her usual self, pretty much. I'm so happy to see her this way. The sun is shining brightly into the living room and oh, how this so helps both Mom's mood and mine.

Mom's friend Peggy was here with one of her daughters, Susan. She had stopped by to give mom a beautiful porcelain doll. It was a birthstone doll for the month of March. Peggy brought it by for Mom's birthday even though she didn't know when Mom's birthday was for certain. She remembered that it was near the beginning of the year and boy, she was ecstatic to find out that she actually was giving Mom her gift the day before her birthday.

Peggy and Susan couldn't stay long. They had some other things to do but it was really nice of them to stop by. I miss hanging out with them.


March 14th. Today is Mom's fifty-eighth birthday. We have a party planned for her. Roseanne and another lady from Hospice were here today. T has a crush on her. She is a very pretty woman and I couldn't help but to want T to be with someone. He is very lonely and I know how much he wants a girlfriend and someone to share his life with.

While the lady from Hospice was in the bathroom with Mom, washing her up, Alex, Jessica, and a couple of other people helped me decorate the house a bit. We had streamers and balloons. I even made a cake that said "Happy Birthday, Me Ma". Me Ma, is a nickname I had for my mother when I was really young. It was special to me as Mom always liked to tell the story of how, when I wanted out of my crib I would say, "Me Ma. Oh, Me Ma," until she came and got me. I didn't care if anyone else thought the writing on the cake was corny; it wasn't meant for them.

Mom seemed to be doing pretty well today. She liked how we decorated the place. Little did she know how many people were coming over for her birthday. We had a house full. I'm sure Mom was happy to see so many people turn out for her birthday but I was both happy and sad. I was happy that so many could come but sad in that I have never seen this many people show up for her birthday before. Why is it that when a person is dying that everyone decides they can show up? Why do they wait so long? Why can't they show up when a person is healthy and spend time with them; give the person a chance to cherish the memory for years to come instead of only weeks.

I could only imagine what Mom must be feeling with all this noise going on. She has been looking rather pale and distraught lately. She is really going downhill and she tends to be slowly drifting away.

The house full of family and friends, was in all, a joyous occasion. Yet, while everyone chit chatted in the living room with Mom, I was out in the kitchen finishing the last decorative touches on the cake. Dad came into the kitchen and told me to hurry as Mom was sore from sitting in her chair and she just wanted to lie down. I hurried and put the candles on the cake. Dad then took the cake into the living room before I was ready. I went to get the camera so I could take a picture of Mom's reaction as she saw the cake.

Did he wait? No. I ended up missing Mom's reaction and her blowing out the candles. Everyone else got to see it and so have that memory but I don't. I was left out, which was how I tended to feel ever since I was young and my nieces and nephews got to go places but somehow, there just never seemed to be enough room for me. I would end up staying home with Mom and she often saw how hurt I was and managed to cheer me up.

Now it was my turn to cheer her up with the cake, but unfortunately, I was in the wrong room to be able to capture her surprise. I'm sure I will never be able to get that moment back.

Guess I'm still not sure how I feel about Mom having cancer and all. Lately I've been having a clear mind about it because I won't allow myself to think too deeply about it. I don't want to anyway. Why? Because I don't want to get dragged down, for fear that I'm not sure I'd come out of it. I cry when I feel I can't hold it back any more. So many people say I can call and talk to them about anything, but there are so many people to choose from. I'm just overwhelmed. I'm getting exhausted with having to help Ma both day and night, but I love her with all my heart and more. I will do anything for her even if I am getting tired. Hopefully, with the way I am handling this situation it won't cause me problems in the long run, but I just don't know how else to handle it.

March 24th. When Dad or someone cries about Mom and I don't, I feel bad, maybe even guilty because I'm not crying. What do I do? Start to cry too? It's not that I don't have feelings about this situation because I do. Everything has happened so fast it hasn't sunk in yet. I'm also three months behind comprehending things than others. Not all things take me that long to comprehend. With all of this—it may. I also was born with a condition which when people hesitate to do something, I hesitate more than they do. It takes me longer to do certain things. I guess I'm hesitant to believe what's happening. I feel like this is a dream, but everyday I keep waking up to it. I know it is real.

Beth came over and saw Mom today. Teka was happy to see Beth and gave her all sorts of kisses. Dad walked Beth into the living room to Mom's bedside. I was nervous with Beth and Dad being in the same room together as I knew they had their differences. Still, I'm glad Beth decided to come. I was relieved to see her.

Beth knelt by Mom's bedside; "That's just too early," she said quickly standing up. I gave her a strange look, but I wasn't sure what she meant. I didn't see a problem with kneeling beside Mom. I wondered if people did this at the calling hours and that's why she said that. Anyway, Beth visited with Mom for a bit before, she had to leave. I walked Beth outside to the car where Robby and Elaine, Beth's sister and brother-in-law, and her mother-in-law, Art were waiting for her.

Then when Margie came home and saw me hugging Beth in the driveway today...She barely gave us notice and rushed on into the trailer. Oh, but how two sisters came to be at odds is truly another story...a story that should have been left in the past long ago. The past is the past after all and *if* they could just live their *present* lives, I think they would both be happier. Life is something too short to fuss after. It just makes it harder for me to deal with Ma's situation and to have to deal with two feuding sisters.

March 25th. I'm worried about Dad. What will happen to him? What will he be like after? Will he act like I'm not even here because he's so wrapped up in his own feelings? What will happen to me then? I'm only seventeen and I'm not quite ready to go out into the world yet. But I guess there is no "ready", is there?

*But when Jesus heard this, He said, "This sickness is not to end in death, but for the glory of God so that the Son of God may be glorified by it." ~ John 11:4 NASB*


## CHAPTER 7

### DEARLY DEPARTED


Mom is about to leave us. I know that but I don't want to believe it. Should be any day now.

Ron, the Hospice nurse, was here today to check up on Mom. It was early afternoon when he arrived and while he jotted stuff down, a few family members chatted briefly with Ma and gave her hugs. I think it was Dad who came to me after he gave Mom a hug and told me that she wanted to see me. I went to Mom's bedside and she very weakly held her arms up, ready to embrace me in a hug. I bent over her and gently wrapped my arms around her; her now thin arms rested lightly upon my back.

"I love you, Mom," I said in a gentle voice.

"I love you too," she replied and then loosened her arms and dropped them to her sides.

I broke away from her in a flood of tears and someone held me. I cannot even remember who it was I was so distraught.

So many people, both family and friends, were here today. I cannot even count how many there were. Most were friends from Fellowship Baptist Church who knew our family very well. They had come to see Mom and to pay their respects. Most of the time Mom was asleep. She was on such a high dose of pain medication she was often asleep. Yet, the pain patches she was using are not

46

working like they used to. She was switched to liquid morphine that is to be given to her by an eye dropper.

It was such a late night I can barely even remember how it ended. There was just so much commotion going on. Our farm house is a good size but with the amount of people that were here it seemed tight sometimes, which isn't good for me. I tend to be a bit claustrophobic.

Though I was happy to have everyone at the house, I was relieved when the crowd dispersed and I could go to bed. I lingered in the living room before going upstairs to my room. Mom wasn't doing so well. Her breathing is very labored and I watch her to see if she is going to take another breath. It's painful to watch her but I feel anxiety more than anything. I just know that soon she won't be taking another breath and I feared when that time would come. I was getting tired and desperately needed to go to bed and it took the coaxing and reassuring words of my family members to help me find peace enough to go to bed.

Thankfully, I can sleep in my own bed as Aunt Margie and Uncle Ronnie, Aunt Art and Margie stayed with Mom. That way Dad and I could both get some much-needed rest.

I was up on and off through the night. I just kept wondering how close Mom was to leaving us. I kept listening for the hum of the oxygen machine and as long as I heard it, I knew Ma was still alive. I feared Mom would leave us soon and all I could do was wait in the silence and dimness of my room.


April 8th. I was up in the early morning. I couldn't sleep. When I went to bed last night Mom wasn't breathing so well. Her pain was so great she wasn't on the Darvocet, or pain-killer patches, anymore. She's was on liquid Morphine. Since she's been taking it, she has been able to sleep better. In fact, that's mostly what she has been doing.

It is kind of stormy this morning. Margie, Aunt Margie, Uncle Ronnie and I think Aunt Art were downstairs with Ma. Dad and I were able to sleep in our own beds last night. Though I don't think either one of us got too much sleep. At least I didn't. All I could think of is the day when someone would come to me and tell me Mom had passed. It was about 5 or 5:30 when I awoke to a storm. I was too afraid to get out of bed and go see Mom. I was afraid she would die in front of me and I didn't know how I would handle that.

So I stayed in bed and listened to the fading storm outside. I had a strange feeling that I had never had before during a storm. As the storm faded, I felt like Mom's spirit was taken away with the storm.

Then when all was quiet weather-wise, I heard talking downstairs and then footfalls ascending the stairs. Whoever was walking upstairs made their way through Beth's old bed room and to Dad's door. There was a knock and, "Dad?" It was Margie. She got Dad's attention and I heard her tell him that Mom had passed. It was now six AM. I heard Dad stirring in his room and then footsteps making their way to my door. There was a knock and, "Jan?" Margie opened the door and I sat up in bed. She told me mom had just passed and I sat there on my bed with my head down as she left the room. I already knew before she told me.

Surprisingly, I didn't cry. I felt an inner peace that I thought was out of place. How could I possibly be at peace? My mother had just died. Yet, I understood the peace I felt. Mother wasn't in pain anymore and she was at rest, never to endure earthly hardships again.

I quickly got dressed and went down stairs, not fully believing my mother was gone. When I walked into the living room I half expected her to still be breathing but she wasn't. I stood there, frozen, watching the stillness of my mother's body. I kept pleading for her stomach to rise and fall as if I could will her breathing to start again with a mere thought. Her stomach never moved and stayed in a fixed position. Reality sunk in with a fierce blow and the emotion I felt building within me exploded in large, body-wracking sobs.

My Aunt Margie held me and I cried hard until I just couldn't cry out everything I was feeling. There was just so much emotion and thought inside me I felt I might explode.

Ron showed up from Hospice and he went in the living room to clean Ma up and make some phone calls. While he did so I waited out in the kitchen with Margie, my two aunts and my uncle. Phone calls were made there as well to alert other members of the family about Mom's passing. I hadn't told anyone yet and so when the phone was free, I managed to snatch it and call my sister Beth. Her husband answered the phone but quickly handed Beth the phone. I told her about Mom but I was too late. Alex had just told her.

Car after car lined the road as people found out that Mom had passed away. I remember staring out the window at the road as Joel and his wife Kylie pulled up alongside the road. I had never seen a car stop so fast before and it surprised me. They zipped in and instantly halted. Everything seems to slowly become more real...

A short while later, Roseanne showed up and she was lost somewhere in the crowd. Ron, Alex, Robby, Jessica and I were standing out in the driveway when the hearse from the TLC Funeral Home pulled in. Matt, had gone to school regardless of what had happened. I couldn't understand how he could to go school after his Grandmother had just died. But then I realized it may be too much for him to stay here and face it. I think it was his way of dealing with it. I may never know the true answer.

I believe it was Ron who called Joann Ives from the TLC Funeral Home just down the road from where we live. The funeral home used to be The Mill Creek Bar and Restaurant but that seemed like forever ago.

I watched as Mom, covered by a sheet, was wheeled out of the house on the stretcher. She was carried down the stairs and then placed in the back of the hearse. The door was closed and Mom was driven away. It was real now... She was gone... Literally taken away from the home...away from...the family life she so loved...away from me. My mother was gone and I was numb with emotion, uncertain with how to feel and how to handle everything I was feeling. I was relieved she was no longer in pain and would never have to face hardships again, yet I was sad and wished I could be in a warm sunny field somewhere where everything was peaceful and happy.

About an hour passed before Roseanne and a few other people were standing on the back porch chatting away. I was

49

talking with Roseanne while slightly shivering; the sun was making its way to the south side of the house, its warmth slowly creeping over the back yard.

"For a while I had a feeling someone wasn't going to make it to my eighteenth birthday and sometimes I thought it would be me," I said, unsure if Roseanne would believe me. I looked into her deep brown eyes and admired her long, dark brown curly hair falling over her shoulders.

"Why did you think it would be you?" She gazed at me in concern.

"Because I didn't want anyone else to die."

Roseanne's face softened and she understood where I was coming from.

The rest of the day was mostly a blur. So many people where there including Mom's friend Peggy. Peggy has two daughters Susan and Sandra but I can't remember if she brought both of them with her or not. Peggy was crying as she walked in to see Dad and say a few words. She wasn't here long at all and I can't say as I blame her. I was learning how hard it was to go through the loss of a loved one.

There came a time I just had to get away. I needed to take a walk. Robby went with me. We walked up to the corner and talked most of the way. I'm having a hard time remembering what we talked about but I'm sure some of what we said was reminiscent of Mom and how we couldn't believe she was gone.

Our neighbor, Mrs. Wadsworth, lived on the corner of Sulpher Springs Road and Massey Street. She must have seen us walking and came out to see us. She asked how Mom was doing and we told her that she had passed early this morning. Her face deepened with sadness and she said, "Oh. I'm sorry." We said a few more words and Robby and I started our walk back to the house.

On our way back, my brother Joel was walking up the road to greet us. When we met up, he asked me if I knew where the cross necklace Alex gave Mom was. Alex wanted the necklace back. I told Joel I knew where the necklace was and so we hurried back.

I wound my way through the maze of people in the house, the most bodies I have ever seen in the house. I went into the dining room, to the small cabinet with an ironing board attachment by the roll-top desk. I opened the cabinet door and pulled out a small white box. I opened the box and there was a bunch of jewelry some of it broken. Resting in a bed of fluffy white cotton was the multicolored gem necklace Alex bought Mom. I gave the necklace to Joel.

Many relatives were here at the house and there were so many. Some of them I had never met before. Mom's brother Andy was here from Florida and I don't remember him at all. Her step-father, Grandpa Albert was also here and he came from West Edmunston, NY. I'm not even sure where that is. It was good to see him again. I think the last time I saw him was after Grandma Albert, his wife, died in October of 1991, eight years ago. Wow! Sure has been a long time.

Tilly, Mom and Dad's friend who was deaf and mute, was there. She was sitting on the wicker couch with a couple of other people with her. She was upset about something. I think I may have asked what was wrong but I'm not sure. I did find out that she was upset over losing her Rosary. She had it last when she was in the bathroom. I had to use the bathroom anyway, and after I was done and had washed my hands, I looked all over the bathroom for the Rosary. I couldn't find it laying on top of anything so I crouched down on my hands and knees and found it under the towel rack. I was happy to have found it for Tilly as I know how much a symbol of someone's religion can mean to them. I walked out of the bathroom and handed Tilly the Rosary. Her face lit up with a smile and grateful eyes. She thanked me in words as best as she could. I told her she was welcome.

The day went on all crazy like with the house full of people and my room was even full. It was evening and I was in my room playing music on my stereo. Jessica, our cousin Korrie, my friends Charlene, Heather, my nephew (by marriage) Branson and Matt were in my room just hanging out. I think my friend Katie might have been there as well but I'm not sure. It's hard to remember after seeing so many faces during the day.

Heather ended up going home. I think she was having a hard time handling everything and that is okay. I know it couldn't have been easy for her seeing me go through grief and trying to hide it under a persona of a mellow mood.

For a couple of hours, we listened to music and then played regular Nintendo. Matt and Branson ended up leaving at some point. I don't know what time Jessica, Charlene, Korrie and I went to bed but I was the first one asleep. The others stayed up a bit longer but I was wiped out. I know if I didn't have friends and family staying with me, I wouldn't be dealing with this so calmly. They were such a comfort to me and they don't know how much I appreciated them staying over.

Sometime in the middle of the night I had to get up and use the bathroom. First I had to climb over the bodies on my floor to get to the door. I descended the stairs and the closer I got to the doorway leading into the dining room, fear set in that I might run into Mom's spirit. She did die in the house after all and I was not too sure what to think, having never personally dealt with the death of someone I loved so much.

I was half awake as I stepped into the dining room and then into the paneled room. There in the room was my sister Margie talking with our brother Edward and his wife Monica. They scared me at first as I wasn't expecting them to be there and then once I realized who they were, I walked right over to Edward and buried myself in his arms. I gave him a hug and then went to the bathroom. Somehow, I made it back upstairs and into bed. I threw the covers over me and I quickly went back to sleep.

*Charm is deceitful and beauty is vain,*
*But a woman who fears the Lord, she shall be praised.*
*Proverbs 31:30 NASB*


# CHAPTER 8

## SAYING GOOD BYE


April 10th. The first day of calling hours is today and I don't know how I will deal with everything. The calling hours are four to six and seven to nine. I heard that usually when people die there is only one day of calling hours but because Mom knew so many people there will be calling hours tomorrow too as many people were coming from out of state and they wouldn't be here until tomorrow. This made me realize how special Mom was to everyone that she warranted two sets of calling hours. I was already proud of her because of the loving and caring life she lived, but now I am even more proud of who she was. I am so thankful I had her for a mother.

Most of the afternoon was spent with my friends Katie, Charlene and Heather. When it came time for the calling hours, everyone at the house, and there were many, rushed around to get ready. It was a sunny day out today, though the wind by dusk, was quite chilly. My friends and I decided we would walk to the funeral home. I needed time to prepare myself to see Mom in the state she was in for the second time. A car ride would prove too short. The walk would be about a mile but that didn't stop us any.

While we were on our walk, my cousin Eileen passed in a van but she slowed down and reversed the van until she met up with us. She asked us if we wanted a ride but I told her we were fine and she drove off.

Once at the funeral home entrance my friends went in first as I hung back, reluctant to go in because I didn't know how I would react and I didn't know how I would handle seeing Mom in a casket.

In the entry hall, there were two, well I guess they were doormen, letting people in and greeting them. There was also a guest book to sign and "In Memoriam" cards for people to take. I let my friends go first and then I walked into the room where Mom was lying in state.

It happened. Just like I thought it would. I glanced at Mom who, unexpectedly was right in my line of sight, and I was overwhelmed so quickly and forcefully with emotion I wailed. My body trembled and I thought I would drop to my knees. Everyone's attention was on me and I didn't care. I knew they understood.

I cried in my hands, only hoping and wishing someone would come and hold me so I could "cry on their shoulder'" so to speak. Alex stepped forward and held me, my sobs muffled by his chest.

"It's okay, Jan. Just let it out," he said, reassuring me that I needn't be ashamed to cry.

He held me for a few minutes and he asked me if I wanted Beth to hold me. I told him I did. I didn't even know she was there. In fact, I didn't know who all was there besides my friends as Mom was the first one I saw when I walked into the room. Everyone else was hanging out to the sides of the room, leaving the path to Mom wide open and clear.

It didn't take long for Alex to find our sister Beth and she came over to comfort me. There was so much inside me I wanted to cry out but I couldn't cry hard enough to relieve all of my pain. I wanted to, but the energy just wasn't in me.

At one point, one of my sisters, I can't remember now if it was Margie or Beth...I think it was Margie...but she asked me if I wanted to go up and see Mom. I told her I did and Alex walked with us.

My heart sank and my stomach lurched when I saw Mom. She was pretty and looked healthy even. But there was a problem. She was all done up in make-up and part of me protested, "That's not my mother. She never wore make-up." I said something to this effect out loud and my sister told me they dressed her all up because if they didn't Mom would probably be all pale and so sickly looking it would shock everyone.

My sister then told me it was okay to touch Mom but she did warn me that she was cold. Even though she told me this it was still hard to fathom. Mom cold? Nah. It seemed impossible but I knew it was true.

I slowly reached out my semi-shaky hand and touched Mom. I wasn't going to at first but I knew I would regret it and wish I had later. This was my last time to touch my mother and I was going to take this opportunity no Matter how hard it would be or how scared I was.

My sister was right. I flinched at Mom's ice-cold skin. I felt my brows furrow as if I didn't understand. Perhaps I didn't. Maybe I still don't. How could she be so cold? She was just alive a few days ago. I understand the concept of death but no Matter how often it is explained to me I can't quite grasp the reality of it. How can someone just be gone when the memory of their life and how they touched you is still so real? It is a dizzying cycle.

Alex knelt on the small alter in front of Mom and grabbed the hand that I had held. He talked to her like she was still alive. I envied him for how he could do so. Though I wanted to talk to Mom, I couldn't bring myself to do it. I know why people talk to their deceased loved ones and it's because of the belief they can still hear you. But...here I was and I couldn't do it. Mother was gone. In all scientific sense, she couldn't hear me, so why would I try to talk to her?

When I had all I could bare of standing next to Mother, I stepped away to allow other people a chance to say good bye. I hadn't realized until after I walked away from Mom how many people had arrived. The small room was almost packed but I was

55

able to get a look of all of the flowers set up around Mom and there was even a photo room divider set up that was made of wood and glass. Behind the glass, in the different sized and segregated frames were pictures of various stages of Mom's life and other pictures of the family. It was really a nice set up and I was pleased with it. The only thing I didn't like about the calling hours was the overwhelming smell of the flowers. They made me nauseous as they made me remember Grandma Albert's funeral and the smell of her flowers. Ever since Grandma Albert's calling hours I never liked the smell of such a large group of flowers.

The rest of the calling hours from four to six and seven to nine were uneventful. Just family members and friends coming in to pay their respects and chat with family and friends they haven't seen in a long time.

April 11th. The second day of calling hours went better than the first. Well, it was emotionally easier but I think it's because I'm really too drawn out to cry.

My former English teacher, Mr. Hand, from Sackets Harbor High was here. My class even sent a bouquet of flowers to the funeral home. This shocked me. I wasn't expecting them to do that. It was such a nice gesture and I'll never forget it.

I even saw one of my classmates, Mikey, and his mother, Patty. I was happy to see them and a little surprised. I knew they knew me and my parents but I still wasn't expecting to see them. They also had a foreign exchange student with them. I think his name was Shinn and he is cute.

Ron from Hospice stopped in and he hung out with me and my friends. He is a comical guy and he made us laugh. With all this sadness and uncertainty going on, laughing seemed almost like a distant memory.

Both sets of time designated for calling hours were pretty much the usual paying respects and all. Nothing outstanding really happened that I decided to write about.

April 12th. The funeral service is today at Fellowship Baptist Church. But first everyone is going the TLC Funeral Home for the memorial service. Many family members and friends of the family showed up as the time for the memorial service grew closer.

Everyone was getting ready and the limos began to arrive. The family is to ride in limos from the house to the funeral home but I didn't want to ride in one. I figured someday I would ride in a limo and I wanted my first memory riding in one to be unassociated with death. I was also reaching my limit on how much of this situation I could handle and decided not to go to the memorial service.

Beth and a couple of others in the family asked me if I was riding in a limo and I told them, "No." I had forgotten to tell Beth that I had decided not to go to the memorial service at the funeral home. Instead I would ride with my cousin Eileen, my Aunt Art, my friends Charlene, Katie and Heather to the church where we would wait for everyone.

We arrived at Fellowship Baptist Church on Arsenal Street, across from the Salmon Run Mall, rather early. My friends and I sat in the pews for quite some time and the time for the funeral service was rather close, yet no one except the people I arrived with, were at the church. I felt like something was wrong. I think it was Eileen's cell phone that rang and I looked back at her in time to see her look at me and say into the phone, "Yes, she's here."

After she hung up the phone I found out why everyone was taking so long. Everyone at the funeral home was looking for me. I felt horrible and even scared that Dad or other family members might be mad at me for having forgotten to tell them I wasn't going to the memorial service. They knew I wasn't riding in a limo, but they still thought I was going to the memorial service.

While my friends and I were waiting, I told my Aunt Art that we were going to go for a walk next door to KMart. I didn't think she was going to let me go at first but she did. So Katie, Charlene, Heather and I went to KMart to pass some time. By the time we got out of there and stepped into the parking lot, we had a pretty good view of the church parking lot and it was filling up with all sorts of vehicles.

We rushed quickly across the two parking lots and I was trying hard not to jog right out of my shoes as they were Katie's and a bit too big for me, but they went good with my outfit. We made it to the church and in the lobby I was confronted by, I think

57

his name was Scott Coolie, and he told me about where my family would be sitting. I was to sit on the left side of the main room while my friends sat on the right side.

I sat alone for a while before a large amount of people poured into the church. My cousins Eileen, Andrea, and a few others were sitting in the pew directly behind mine, and there were a few people ahead of me. Yet there was no on beside me. I looked at my friends just across the way and they kept asking me if I wanted them to sit with me. It's not that I didn't want them to, but the seating was arranged and so I thought I would be messing it up if I had them sit with me.

I stared at the center of the room where the aisle was and watched as my mother's coffin was brought into the room and up to the front. Eileen asked me if I would be okay. I shook my head and broke down crying as an overwhelming ball of emotion broke within me. Thankfully, Eileen came up and sat beside me to offer me comfort.

Dad came down the aisle in deep, verbal sobs, with one person on each side of him, steadying him as he walked to his seat. I had never seen Dad so emotional and it scared me. The last time I remember seeing him anything like this was when his mother, Mona Monroe, or Grandma Monroe as I called her, died in 1987. I was sad then and at five, going on six, I barely understood what was happening then.

I continued to watch the aisle and then saw my brothers and sisters and a few of my nieces and nephews walk into the room. The walked up to the first couple of pews on the *right* side of the room and sat down. *Why were they on the right side of the room*, I thought. *I was told to sit on the left side of the room. Why are they are on the right?*

I was getting nervous and anxious thinking that I would be totally separated from my family while going through this service. When I saw Beth, I calmed down a bit and stared at her with pleading eyes. She didn't see me as her back was to me but Eileen noticed my reaction. "Do you want me to see if Beth will come over here and sit with you?"

"Yes," I said feeling a sense of relief as Beth was the next one to Mom that I was closest to in the family.

I watched Eileen walk over to Beth. Eileen pointed Beth in my direction and she quickly came to my side. If I remember correctly, Beth had told me that she was looking for me and that she really didn't feel comfortable sitting with anyone else in the family. In the years prior, Beth had been going through quite a bit and I had been the only one in the family who really stuck by her through everything. I know that is why we felt the closest to each other.

With pews full and people loitering in what aisle and lobby room they could find, the service commenced. I believe the Pastor who opened the service with a few words was Pastor James. I'm not sure though. My mind is becoming all jumbled with everything and it is hard remembering faces after seeing so many in the past few days.

There were a number of tributes read to Mom written by her children and grandchildren, but they were read by members of the church as we couldn't quite find the strength to read the tributes ourselves. Among the tributes read were a poem by my brother Joel; a poem "About My Mother-In-Law" by Monica, my brother Edward's wife; "Forever My Mother" a poem I wrote just about a week before Mom's death; Matt had the Guns 'n' Roses' lyrics to "Don't Cry" read, which I found were very appropriate. I wasn't too sure at first until I heard the words. Then there was a tribute by Jessica. She had recorded herself singing "Wind Beneath My Wings" on cassette and had it played back. That song was Mom and Dad's song. There was a large response to the song and in a way I was jealous. Jessica was always treated better than I was and had been ever since we were very little. I always felt she was a few rungs higher than I was and more revered and praised when she did something good. I don't know if that was true perception or not but that is how I always felt.

My poem "Forever My Mother" was read by Laura Simpson, the daughter of Mr. and Mrs. Simpson who are very good friends of Mom and Dad's. She had a hard time reading it through her sobs. I broke down crying the full reality of my words now true since Mother's passing. I had been crying pretty much the whole time she read my poem that I never heard the full reaction of the crowd. I heard a few sniffles here and there but that was it.

After Laura finished reading my poem, I heard from both Eileen and Beth that there had been a large response to my poem. Many people had broken out in tears and sniffles. This shocked me at first and at the same time made me feel good that maybe, just maybe I was just as recognized as Jessica. I started not to feel so invisible anymore.

I don't quite remember exactly what happened after all of the tributes were read, but I think it was the Rose Ceremony. Each of Mom's children were to pick up a red rose and lay it in her casket as a way of saying that we love her and telling her good bye. I had no idea this was going to happen and when I heard this my body began to shake. *Can I do this? I don't know if I can. This is getting to be too much!* I thought, walking shakily up to the front and over to the right side of the room. Dad was in the front pew and his red, tear stained face lit up a bit when he saw me. I gave him a long hug before I was handed a long stemmed, red rose.

I believe it was in the order of our birth that each of six kids laid a rose beside Mom who looked at peace and just as beautiful as I remember her. Mom never wore make-up that I saw, so she looked pretty, but different than I was used to. She appeared as though she was sleeping, yet if I touched her I knew there would be no heat in her and the utter reality would course through my emotionally weakened body once again.

Down through the line it went: Edward, Margie, Alex, Joel, Beth...and then me. My turn to leave a rose with my mother. After Beth stepped away from the casket,

I stepped up to it with shaky knees I felt were ready to buckle. As I laid the rose next to Mother, her hands resting on her stomach, I felt something rise inside me. It was a feeling of warmth and comfort that spoke to me saying, "Even though she will shortly be gone out of your site, she will never fully leave you."

I couldn't take it anymore. The feeling was comforting but my sadness didn't abate and only rose knowing that this was the last time I would see my mother's face and be able to touch her. I tried to hold back the sob building in my throat but it defeated me and I had to leave the room. Beth took a hold of me and we left by the side aisle on the left side of the room and out into the foyer. I lingered there for a while as the service continued and I gradually calmed down enough to where Beth and I could return to our seats.

It wasn't long after that the service came to a close and the departing words were that of instruction to the cemetery for the graveside ceremony.

As we departed the church and entered the parking lot, I looked around me and could not believe the amount of cars, trucks and vans that crowded the parking lot and even the lawn. I don't know who Beth rode with, but my friends and I rode with my cousin Eileen and her mother, my Aunt Art.

From the church parking lot we drove down Arsenal Street and after that I'm not sure what roads we took. I'm a total country girl and I know my way around the country setting fairly well, but if you take me into the city forget it. I know how to get to certain stores and streets, but the route we were taking was alien to me, or so it seemed. We were going to the Maple Hill Cemetery, in Rutland, NY which is where Grandma Albert, my mom's mom, was buried in 1991. I didn't know how to get there then and I don't now.

The ride seemed like it lasted for about half an hour but I'm not sure that it was even that long. It might have been though with the traffic on Arsenal. Every so often on the drive, I would look out the back window and look at the row of cars in the procession. There were so many cars and the line was so long I could not count the cars as they all seemed to run together toward the end of the line. Again, I realized how important my mom was to so many people. Because of her Godly caring and loving nature, she touched so many lives. I want to be like her. I want to be there as she was for all my loved ones and anyone else who may need me. I want to have a lot of people at my funeral too.

Once in Rutland, I recognized the long winding road we were on as it crept up to a large hill. At the top of the hill we turned right, through a black iron gate and passed a small sign that said "Maple Hill Cemetery". I didn't need to read the sign to know where I was. I recognized the place, but not so much from Grandma Albert's funeral. It was exactly as I had seen it in my dreams when I was a child. It was the dream where I was on a hill, in the midst of a cemetery, being led by my sister to my mother's grave. On Mother's gravestone, the outlines of the last three digits of the death year were the same.

That was the dream, yet here I was, in a cemetery, on top of hill, surrounded by the same tall trees, swaying in a cool spring breeze, that were also in my dream. And the last three digits of Mother's death year were the same: 1999.

I know Mom is in Heaven with God, His angels and many other saved people. She once called me a dreamer and since now that she was in Heaven, able to know more than I do, I wondered what she thought of the validity of my dreams now, after once telling me she wasn't going to die. I probably will never know, but I am certain it is a thought I will always have.

There was little room for parking in the cemetery and most everyone had to park in the small grassy area away from the main grave sites. Others parked along the gravel road leading in and out of the cemetery while the rest had to park alongside the main road.

It had been eight years since I had been to this cemetery and I had forgotten where Grandma Albert was buried. To the left end of the cemetery I saw a gathering of people and a green tent which clued me in to where I was supposed to go. My friends and I walked over to the tent and there inside was the metal frame Mom's casket would be laid upon. I'm not sure what the frame thing was called.

Once Mom's casket was lowered on the frame and everyone gathered around was quiet, the graveside ceremony began. A pastor was there to begin and I think it was Pastor James who opened the ceremony. He is a nice man who Mom and Dad have known for many years.

After the ceremony began, anyone who wanted to speak was allowed to. I don't remember what anyone said or even who all spoke as it was all so overwhelming and mentally it is so very hard to take in anymore. I do remember my brother Alex saying a few words and he was very emotional. Out of us six kids, Alex was the only one to display his grief in such an outward fashion. I was too scared to let anyone see how I really felt. I don't know why though because I know there's nothing wrong with crying. Somewhere along the line of growing up, I became afraid to let anyone see my true emotions.

Alex hung out by the casket, with Dad on one side of him and someone else on the other, trying to comfort him and help calm him down. I have never seen Alex so emotional and never knew he cared for Mom so much until now. It broke my heart seeing him that way knowing I couldn't do anything to help him.

The grave side ceremony was shorter than I thought it might be, but then the cold April wind was whipping around us and many of the women had skirts or dresses on. It was damp out as well and I know how troublesome it can be for older people when conditions of cold air and dampness join. I imagine many people were relieved to be able to go home and warm up and put this day behind them.

The next stop after the ceremony was home and how glad I am to be here. Now that all the major dealings are done with, I can settle back a bit and focus on getting through the upcoming days without Mom. It's not easy now and I know it won't be for a while. I am thankful that Edward, Monica and their two boys Lawton and Ian are staying with Dad and me for a while. Life will be easier with them around as I won't be so focused on how I feel about Mom. I am also grateful for my friend Charlene. Out of all my friends she has proven to me to be the only one willing to stay with me indefinitely. With Mom gone I need someone to feel close to and with Charlene I know I can do that and not get hurt in the process. She is a stable, fun-loving, caring and kind person.

Night's will still be hard to handle though as I still fear getting up to go to the bathroom. Can't help but to think Mom will try and scare me. I know it's an irrational thought but with the lack of sleep, or constantly interrupted sleep, coupled with the entire emotional trauma I've been through it's hard to think totally straight. I am full of mixed emotions and thoughts and I don't know where to begin to make sense of them all and I don't know who to talk to about it. Worse yet, even if I did know who I could talk to, I don't know if I could put into words everything I am feeling or thinking. I just don't know what to do.

*Ascribe to the Lord, O sons of the might,*
*Ascribe to the Lord glory and strength.*
*Ascribe to the Lord the glory due to His Name;*
*Worship the Lord in holy array.*

*The voice of the Lord is upon the waters;*
*The God of glory thunders,*
*The Lord is over many waters.*
*The voice of the Lord is powerful,*
*The voice of the Lord is majestic.*
*The voice of the Lord breaks the cedars;*
*Yes, the Lord breaks in pieces the cedars of Lebanon.*
*He makes Lebanon skip like a calf,*
*And Sirion like a young wild ox.*
*The Voice of the Lord hews out flames of fire.*
*The voice of the Lord shakes the wilderness;*
*The Lord shakes the wilderness of Kadesh.*
*The voice of the Lord makes the deer to calve*
*And strips the forests bare;*
*And in His temple everything says, "Glory!"*

*The Lord sat as King at the flood;*
*Yes, the Lord sits as King forever*
*The Lord will give strength to His people;*
*The Lord will bless His people with peace.*
*Psalm 29 NASB*

# CHAPTER 9

## THE AFTERMATH

You might have guessed how my life changed after my mother's death. Here I was seventeen and now had to take on the duties of housewife, cleaning, cooking, laundry, sewing, grocery shopping, etc. And it's not that I knew how to do all those things. Cooking I had to learn by recipes and experimenting, and watching the Food Network, and I knew just the basic stitch for sewing; laundry I had learned a year or so before but I had to remember how to do it since I didn't do it very often.

While doing each of these things, I felt like I was walking in my mother's shoes seeing what she did every day for the family. I realized just how much love and devotion she had for us. I never realized just how much of her energy and time she put into doing everything.

At first doing Mom's work was hard because I'd always remember her doing them and I would break down and cry. It wasn't just the memory of her that made me cry, I also felt overwhelmed and stressed. It was all so much to take on at once. I had no idea how she managed it.

After a while I got used to how things were. Well I got used to Mom's chores but I don't think anyone fully gets used to a loved one being gone. I always feel like she's on vacation and ready to walk through the door any minute.

If anything got me through the loss of my mother and how crazy things seemed afterward it was my faith in God. I just kept trusting and He kept pulling me through one day at a time. He gave me strength when I thought I had none, peace during times it was hard to find, and confidence when I usually felt self-doubt. I'm so grateful my parents taught me about God growing up because knowing Him is what got me through one of the toughest moments of my life.

# ABOUT THE AUTHOR

Janis I. Soucie is a short story, novel writer and poet. Her article "Diabetes and the Celiac Link" was published in the National Health Federation Magazine and website. Her poetry has appeared in several chapbooks by the J.M.W. Publishing Company and has also appeared in a Vermont magazine, EverChanging, and a U.K. magazine Poetic Hours. When she's not writing, you can find her in her kitchen, singing at the top of her lungs while she creates gluten free meals for her family.

Soucie lives in Maine with her family, three parakeets and a chinchilla named Spock.

You can visit her at:
www.jisoucie.com
Twitter: http://www.twitter.com/jisoucie
Instagram: http://www.instagram.com/soucieji

# AUTHOR'S NOTE

This note is just to let my readers know that this book was started in Hyannis, MA at the Comfort Inn, when my husband had to make a business trip for Orvis on December 14, 2005.

I don't know if it Matters much to anyone else but I find it interesting to know where a book was started and then to find out where the author was when it was finished. These records allow you to see where a person has been and perhaps one day you may find yourself in the very same place. I have done so and found it to be exciting. In that respect, from Hyannis, Massachusetts the book began, to Arlington, Vermont, and in our home in Maine, is where it has ended.

I'd love to hear from my fans! Send me an email to jisoucie@hotmail.com.